SPIDER-MAN

DOOM WITH A VIEW

R-MAN

DOOM WITH A VIEW

Writer
Sean McKeever
Pencils
Mike Norton

Inks: **Norman Lee & Jonathan Glapion**
Colors: **Guru eFX's Hartman & Bevard**
Letters: **Dave Sharpe**
Cover Art: **Mike Norton, Jonathan Glapion
& Guru eFX**
Assistant Editor: **Nathan Cosby**
Consulting Editor: **Mark Paniccia**
Editor: **MacKenzie Cadenhead**

Collection Editor: **Jennifer Grünwald**
Assistant Editor: **Michael Short**
Senior Editor, Special Projects: **Jeff Youngquist**
Vice President of Sales: **David Gabriel**
Production: **Jerron Quality Color**
Vice President of Creative: **Tom Marvelli**

Editor in Chief: **Joe Quesada**
Publisher: **Dan Buckley**

#9

Wow! Fasten your seatbelts and make sure your seat trays are in their upright and locked positions, *true believers,* because we're in for one heckuva *bumpy ride!*

That's *Doctor Doom,* the loathsome leader of *Latveria,* who rules his European nation with two iron fists! Doom can hold his own against his greatest enemies, *the Fantastic Four--*

--so what chance does a lone hero like *Spider-Man* have against this *megalomaniacal monarch?* And what are they doing dozens of miles in the air?

HA! Did you think we'd *really* tell you *all that* on page one? Not a chance! So *jet on over to the next page* and get ready for *one turbulent tale!*

DOOM WITH A VIEW!

SEAN McKEEVER
WRITER

MIKE NORTON
PENCILS

NORMAN LEE
INKS

GURU eFX'S HARTMAN and **BEVARD**
COLORS

NORTON, GLAPION and **GURU**
COVER

DAVE SHARPE
LETTERER

BRAD JOHANSEN
PRODUCTION

NATHAN COSBY
ASST. EDITOR

MACKENZIE CADENHEAD
EDITOR

MARK PANICCIA
CONSULTING EDITOR

JOE QUESADA
CHIEF

DAN BUCKLEY
PUBLISHER

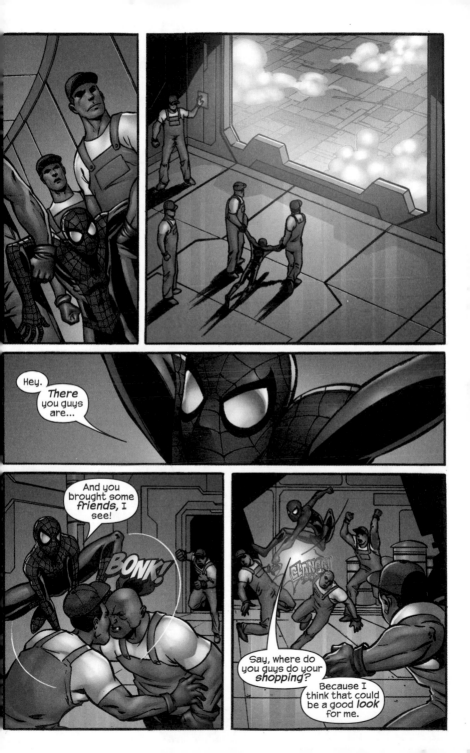

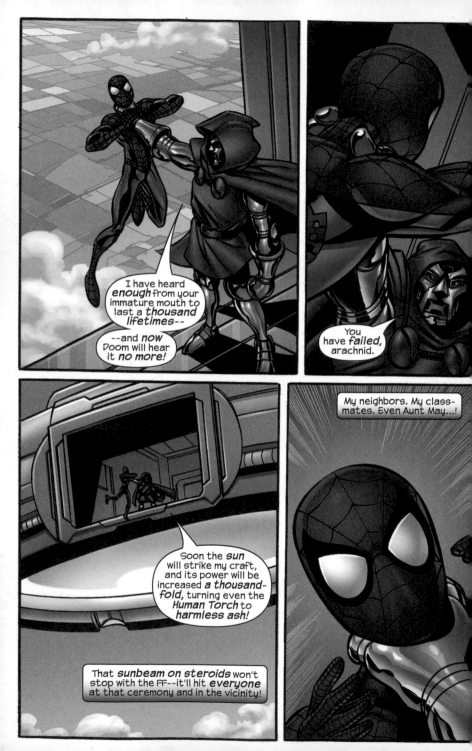

#10

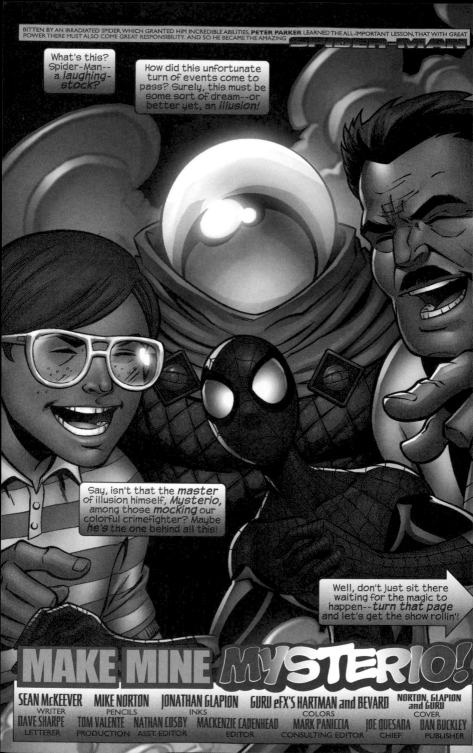

#11

The future! What would you give to know how your life will play out? Or, better yet, to be able to use the knowledge of future events to *make* your life go exactly how you want?

Well, there's a guy who seems to be able to do *just that*--he's called the *Mad Thinker* and he's chosen to *use* his knowledgeable noggin to commit crimes!

Now you're thinking, 'Okay, but what does *any* of this have to do with that *gold robot* kicking Spider-Man's blue behind in front of the *Midtown High* student body?'

That's a great question, True Believers! But to *find out*, you're either going to have to consult your *local fortune-teller* or you can *turn the page* and start reading this stupendous Spidey adventure!

THEY CALL HIM MAD!

SEAN McKEEVER
WRITER

MIKE NORTON
PENCILS

JONATHAN GLAPION
INKS

GURU eFX'S HARTMAN and BEVARD
COLORS

DAVE SHARPE
LETTERER

BRAD JOHANSEN
PRODUCTION

NATHAN COSBY
ASST. EDITOR

MACKENZIE CADENHEAD
EDITOR

MARK PANICCIA
CONSULTING EDITOR

JOE QUESADA
CHIEF

DAN BUCKLEY
PUBLISHER

#12

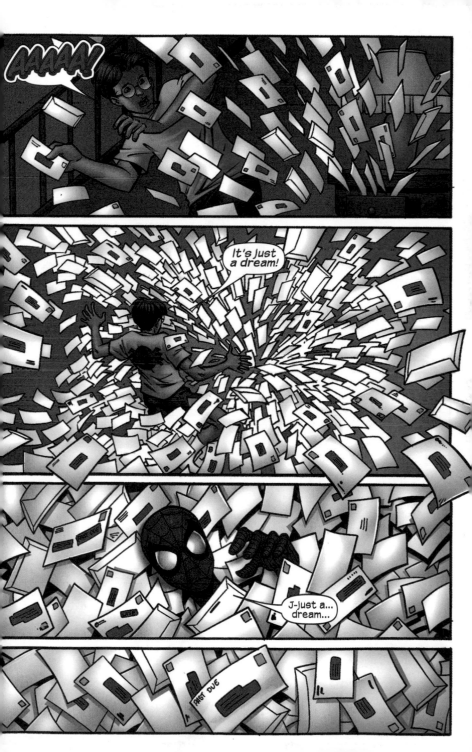